Whose Bad @$$ Kids Are Those?

Whose Bad @$$ Kids Are Those?

A Parent's Guide to Behavior

Jarret "Doctor Jarret" Patton, MD, FAAP

WHOSE BAD @$$ KIDS ARE THOSE?
Published by Purposely Created Publishing Group™
Copyright © 2018 Jarret Patton

All rights reserved.

Printed in the United States of America
ISBN: 978-1-948400-43-5

DEDICATION

This book is dedicated to my wife, Damary, who has supported me throughout this endeavor. She has been my rock and the motivation for this book. Without her, I would not be the parent I am today. Without her, I would not be the man I am today.

I also acknowledge my children and the thousands of patients who have helped me gain wisdom about behavior and parenting.

TABLE OF CONTENTS

INTRODUCTION

Parenting isn't easy. If it were, society would be full of well-behaved children who are self-sufficient and could leave home by the age of 12. But, that is not the case. Depending on your parenting skills, your child may be with you through their teen years and into young adulthood. Therefore, they need your love and support.

Parenting is a huge responsibility. When you think about how important this task is, you wonder why you shouldn't be required to apply for a license and perform some sort of skills test. You might think about that when you walk through the mall and see a group of rambunctious kids. You might even say to yourself, "Whose bad ass kids are those? Glad they aren't mine!" and keep walking.

You put your heart and soul into parenting throughout your lifetime. You want your child to be more successful than you. You want your child to be an independent adult who wins the Nobel Prize in Astrophysics and cures cancer while orbiting Jupiter. This feeling is one reason we may try to give our children too many things, which may have negative consequences.

The current expense of raising a child is nearly $250,000.00 for their lifetime. With an investment like that, why wouldn't you want to see the greatest return? Will your child develop into a kind philanthropist who wants nothing more than to take care of his mother in her middle-aged early retirement? Think of the exercising, fun, and shopping you could do when you are financially free at 50? However, that might be unlikely. You might not see a financial return on your investment, but the love and satisfaction you receive can be quite payment enough.

I am the father of three living children, but that alone does not make me an expert in parenting. I also have over 15 years of pediatric experience. The combination of the two is what makes me a parenting authority. I have watched my own children grow and develop, and each of them does something different than the books say. My daughter is the independent scientist; she lives life through experimentation. My middle child seems to be the textbook example of everything. Of course, my youngest son (the baby) is the exception to every rule.

This book can be read from cover to cover to prepare you for some common challenges that will occur throughout various stages in your child's life. I suggest everyone read chapter one to gain sufficient background information. From there, you can pick and choose the chapter based on the stage of life your child is in. Each chapter is designed specifically with you in mind. You don't have to spend life regretting that you didn't let your teenage daughter "cry it out" as a baby. You can simply go to the "Tweens and Teens" chapter and learn sound advice for what you can do to help correct your child's behavior from this point forward. You will notice several recurring themes throughout this book. For instance, many of the themes discussed in the "Infancy and the First Year" chapter also apply to the "Young Adults" chapter, with different levels of sophistication. These recurring themes are intentional and a part of winning the behavior battle.

All parents and family caregivers are encouraged to read this book. Perhaps you'll want to read it together. This way, you all have the same information and you can discuss where you agree and disagree. Behavior modification is specific to the individual seeking the change. In other words, if only one parent reads the book and implements the suggestion, the behavior change may only work for that parent. The other parent is not armed with the same strategy. Let's face it—your child is smart. They will find ways to undermine the best-laid plan, and ultimately take the path of least resistance (which won't be you).

It is my hope that you enjoy this book. I hope that you find it entertaining and educating. When you apply these principles to your parenting arsenal, you will see a noticeable change in your child's attitude and behavior. These principles aren't for the faint of heart, but sticking to them can transform your child. So, when you hear somebody ask, "Whose bad ass kids are those?" you won't have to look. Instead, you will know with confidence, "Not mine!"

CHAPTER 1
Nature vs. Nurture

The age-old rule of the wild holds true with humans just as it does with lions, dolphins, and eagles; raising children involves both nature and nurture. Unlike a baby zebra that is born and hours later is seen walking and going to feed, humans need a lot more nurturing. However, don't underestimate nature. Your child is benefiting from thousands of years of human existence, which sets the stage for quite a bit of reflexive, yet intentional, actions that will influence your children throughout their lives.

Your child is smart. Humans have the most complex and powerful brains on this planet. From day one, the brain stem (a part of the nervous system beneath the actual brain) has all bodily duties under control. Breathing, eating, and the heartbeat are all being controlled automatically. The brain itself is growing at a fast pace. This is one of the reasons your baby's head is measured at the routine office visits during the first two years of life. This ensures proper brain growth, among other things.

The brain becomes more efficient and powerful over the years. Knowledge about the world is found through discovery. An innate inquisitiveness helps each child learn about their surroundings. Although the brain essentially stops growing after the school-aged years, intelligence never stops building. The more you can help your child discover things about the world, the better off they will be. Sometimes trouble occurs simply from them not knowing the dangers of a situation. For instance, sticking a finger in the electrical outlet, jumping on the bed, or experimenting with sex or drugs. Their quest to discover more about the environment around them never ends. Therefore, it is essential that you help explain the world to them through every stage of life.

Basic scientific principles are learned early in life. There is no need to wait until a science class begins. A child will understand the principles of cause and effect in infancy. Crying initially is a reflexive response to a number of things--too cold, too hot, hunger, etc. Babies learn that crying begets a lot of attention. Then, cries start to indicate other things besides the basics like a dirty diaper, pick me up, put me down, I want attention, etc. Instead, crying becomes a learned behavior to get what the baby wants, not necessarily what the parent needs to give.

Although the previous example describes what occurs during infancy, it does not stop there. The same can be said for toddlers, through terrible twos and threes, who have temper tantrums; and, school-aged kids that act out dramatically. Teen tantrums can be tough, but these are learned behaviors that are designed to influence parents to give in.

The influence of nature upon the development of our children is profound. Simple reflexes are innate, and as the brain develops those reflexes become intentional. As parents, our responsibility to our babies makes us confused about their wants and needs. For mothers, the sound of crying prompts the breasts to let down milk to feed the baby. This is not intentional on the mother's part, it is natural. This can be embarrassing when the cute t-shirt you put on becomes wet with milk because you hear some other child crying. It is no wonder Moms have a natural response to crying, and it is directly tied to nature. The problem begins when the natural response is confused with nurture.

As a side note, my response to crying was particularly blunted. My wife often thought I was deaf, as most women think of their husbands and partners. However, I had a double whammy. First, I didn't feel the same response to nature. A baby crying did nothing physiologic to me. Men don't have milk let down or swollen and sore breasts in response to crying. My second problem was that as a pediatrician, I heard children crying all day. To me, the sound of crying was like background noise. I could sleep through a waking baby or ignore a tantrum with ease, as I heard this all day long professionally. I had a great training ground. I ended up tending to my wife's concerns as they were stronger than those of the baby or child. However, I digress…

As parents, nurturing our children is one of our most powerful drives. We want to see that all of their needs are met. We want them to do better than us in life. We want them to have the world. Nurture is a must, as all children do best when they feel love. They ultimately become more secure, have self-soothing behaviors, and feel comfortable with life. We must love our children, but we don't have to spoil them. This is a tough balance especially when we confuse nature and nurture.

The response to nurture also develops very early in life. There are some steps that you can take to help keep your child from taking advantage of you in infancy. However, all is not lost just because you are reading this book during your child's teen years. There are intentional steps that you can take to transform behavior at any age or stage of your children's lives.

Consistency is something that does a lot for a child's wellbeing and has positive effects upon behavior. Being consistent with everything you say and do is what shapes behavior. Regularity is exponentially more powerful when it is practiced as a group rather than individually. That is why it is important that all caretakers read this book and develop a plan of action for behavioral transformation.

Consistency also means that if you threaten punishment or an adverse consequence, you must follow through. The ability of the child to immediately understand the fact that there may not be true consequences to the action can thwart any behavioral modification attempt. This starts in infancy and persists throughout life. You know you can spot, and probably name, a few people at your job or even in your social circle that still act childish.

As children age, they learn by example. The old saying, "Because I said so" does not carry as much weight as it did years ago. If you are not careful, the development of their logical thinking will help them find a way to contradict what you say because research has told us that children react more to what parents do than what we say. This particularly goes for our negative and contradictory behaviors. "Smoking is bad." While you smoke cigarettes. "Don't drink and drive." While you have one last beer before you leave the party. "Wear your bike helmet." As you ride along with your child helmet-less. I am sure you can think of a few more examples of times when you visually contradicted your own rules or lessons. Remember they learn more by reinforcement of what they see than by what they are told.

Finally, understand that transforming your child's behavior is a lifetime process. This is not something that happens overnight. Consistency and good examples can carry you a long way toward the behavior you desire and expect from your kids. Behavior is a long-term commitment. You must decide on the points you wish to enforce.

You must also decide when to retreat. Most of all, I don't want you to be discouraged because you didn't read this book after your baby shower. You must not carry guilt with you. I will repeat this time and time again throughout this book: no guilt. You can only move forward and take corrective action. Read on.

The following chapters will help both you and your child develop skills that will last a lifetime. After all, raising children is a lifelong commitment. The seeds you plant now will be fruitful with time. You will have to pull out weeds now and again to enhance the garden, but the fruit will be sweet. You will watch your child grow and develop into someone who will make you proud. The skills they learn from you, obedience being one of them, will help shape who they become and the impact they make on society. With practice and patience, you are on your way to transformation.

CHAPTER 2

Infancy and the First Year

Infancy is where you can get the most bang for your behavioral buck. If established early and often, the standards you set now will last throughout parenthood. At this time, as we discussed in chapter one, infants are learning about their surroundings. They are transitioning from their comforts in the womb to a cold, bright place with noise and stimuli. This transition is filled with discovery. Meanwhile, the behavior of your baby is actively being formed.

They quickly learn that their sole form of communication is crying. In fact, a baby that never cries may indicate a medical problem and should be evaluated by your physician. They will cry for diapers, food, warmth, and attention. Heck, they will cry because they are crying. Within the first two months of life, you must use your investigative powers to determine what your baby is communicating. It could be for any of the previous reasons. Needless to say, nature and nurture can be confused because of the crying behavior. However, with time, you will become in tune with your baby's communication.

During the first few months, you can do whatever it takes to settle your baby. There is no such thing as spoiling. In fact, during this time a baby learns that their needs will be met which makes them secure. This sense of security will lay the foundation for better behavior in the future.

It is also important to establish a schedule with your baby, who will likely feed on demand during the first several weeks. Breast fed babies tend to eat more often. However, you will soon see the feed, poop, sleep cycle become established if you allow baby to develop a schedule. This means that you must be aware that babies sleep up to 19 hours a day and they need that sleep. With time, their sleep needs decrease and the feeding intervals increase, especially after solid foods are introduced between four and six months of age. Remember that all babies should be placed on their backs to sleep.

Raising and breastfeeding a baby can be a lot of work; so, during the first two to three months, you must be in check with your emotions. With your sleep schedule so often interrupted, your wellbeing can be at risk. Post-partum depression can cause significant debilitation to your functioning, which carries over to your baby's well-being. "Baby blues" (frequent feelings of sadness) are also common. Your obstetrician and pediatrician should be screening you for these conditions during you or your baby's office visits. If you feel that you are being affected, call your physician.

During the next three to four months, you will really know the personality of your child. You will know if you have a happy baby, a fussy baby, or a relaxed baby. It is at this stage that you should consider letting your child cry if there are no immediate needs. Letting your baby cry will allow them to develop self-soothing skills, which leads to better problem solving later in life. Your schedule should be well established since you can now anticipate the needs of the child. Don't fall for that shriek or that trembling lip. They will also learn to give you that, "Mommy, don't you love me anymore?" look. These are skills of negotiation developing.

It is important for you not to feel guilt during these early stages of infancy. You are doing everything you can to feed, clothe, and keep your baby clean. Don't let the crying get to you. If you continually pick up and soothe an older baby, it could lead to dependency and open the door for worse outbursts in the future.

Keeping this "no guilt" mantra in mind, realize that mommy and daddy's receptors to crying are different. Mothers have a physiological response to crying, which causes them to have milk let down. This can make it more difficult for a mother to ignore crying. As a result, you must be vigilant and aware of these responses and know that it is ok to ignore crying when it appears to be for no reason. Don't blame fathers because they don't seem to mind the crying as much. In fact, I would often get in trouble at home with my wife as she would respond quickly to crying and I would barely notice that our son was making any noise. After all, nurture and nature can be easily confused at this stage as the response to anything is very likely crying.

At around four months of age, solid foods can safely be introduced. You will do yourself a big favor now and later if you keep a wide variety of foods in your baby's diet. You will certainly notice that even at this young age they will prefer some variety. However, if you stop giving them the foods they don't like now, it sets the stage for extremely picky eating later. If you hang tough and do not give into the "yuck face," they will continue to eat a wider variety of foods while appreciating healthier choices. In the first eight to nine months, the main source of nutrition should be breast milk or formula, so nutritionally speaking, having small amounts of solid foods doesn't matter.

Around the six-month milestone, you should get rid of the pacifiers. Some babies are very dependent on these pacifiers and others could care less. However, to keep your baby's teeth growing in correctly, it is important to stop pacifier usage. This is something that can be difficult as the pacifier dependent babies really get mad when they can't get their fix. There is only one surefire way to get rid of the pacifiers––round them all up and throw them away. Put them out on garbage day and don't turn back. Your sweet child will cry seemingly endlessly for the pacifier. Hang tough. No guilt. Within a few days, the pacifier will be forgotten. After all, you don't want your child to be that four-year-old with a pacifier hanging out of their mouth.

Finally, remember that the brain is growing and developing at a significant pace now. Your child is getting smarter by the day, and learning to adapt to surroundings and manipulate them. Early on, although not fully mobile, your child knows how to get you to move for them. Know that through these early months of life, their manipulation and negotiation skills are developing. However, don't be afraid to set limits. Limit setting will go a long way toward establishing expectations for your child as their verbal communication continues to develop over their first two years of life.

You are not alone in this journey. You will have frequent visits with your baby's doctor. This allows you time to check in with yourself and determine if you are on the right track. These visits help verify the baby's proper growth and development. Make a list of questions and discuss them at the visit to give you a better time experience.

Setting the tone in the first few months of life will carry you through the infancy stage into the toddler years. Establishing a schedule and letting the child find their own solutions to the problem will pave the way for better behavior throughout the toddler years, as well as the terrible twos and threes. Also, stay in tune with your own feelings and emotions so that you can be the best parent possible.

CHAPTER 3

Toddlers Through "The Terrible Twos, Threes, and Fours"

So far, parenting is a breeze, right? You have soared through that first year of life with ease. You had no problems establishing a schedule or setting limits with your child. You now have the perfect child displaying the perfect behavior. No? Well, remember that parenting is a lifelong obligation and you are only in the beginning. There is still time to improve upon what has been started.

Toddlers through four-year-olds tend to get the worst reputation as far as behavior is concerned. This is attributed to the fact that their brain is still developing and making them smarter. Their verbal and reasoning skills increase. This brings in stronger negotiation skills and a stronger will. They are also known for the dreaded meltdown. This tantrum always occurs in public places and causes extreme embarrassment and potentially guilt, especially if the behavior wasn't put in check during the first year.

After all, in the mind of the child, the world revolves around them. Let's think about it. Up until this point in their life, everything has been done for them and they largely received whatever they wanted. Why would they think anything should change? Therefore, limit setting early on is important. However, if that first year of life was a total disaster, let's move forward and get to catching up with the program.

You are the parent, the boss, and the chief executive officer of your children. You write the rules. You enforce them. You set the tone. Your child will do their best to undermine this system with their intelligence. After all, they are the smartest they have ever been. As a result, kids think that they can outsmart anyone. You must let them know who is in charge by establishing rules and expectations up front.

During these ages, their understanding of verbal commands and their verbal expression increases. However, crying can be a big part of their communication arsenal. They will revert to crying when they don't get their way, especially if crying is tolerated by the parent. This is a good time to start extinguishing "the crying game" by completely ignoring that form of communication. Because the schedule has been well established by this time, you can anticipate the needs before the crying begins. This goes for sleeping, eating, and diaper changing times. Anticipating the needs further solidifies the child's comfort in knowing that all needs will be met. Security of the environment is calming to the demeanor of the child.

This is a perfect time to get the child to further develop their language skills. You can request for your toddler to use the words they are learning to communicate their needs. Simple requests like "food," "eat," "drink," "ba ba," "potty," or "night night" can be effective for the very young child. Reading books to your child daily is essential to furthering their speech development. Just in case it wasn't done earlier, pacifier usage should be discontinued after about six months of age as not to hinder speech or disrupt tooth development. Your child's pediatrician should be monitoring language development. Signs of delayed speech may be displayed through failure to speak or frequent outbursts of crying due to frustration. Although your child should have gotten a hearing screening at birth, hearing difficulties can also arise at this time if speech development does not progress.

As the boss of the children, it is your job to send a message. Early on, your child understands the command "no." As time moves on, they should know that you mean business when you say that word. If they don't listen, you need to immediately reinforce the verbal command with the look of "I ain't playin." They will get both the nonverbal and verbal command. However, you must be consistent with these commands. If not, it opens the door to bargaining and your commands being ignored. You can't let disobedience slide.

Consistency is important throughout this stage of life. If there is no immediate and consistent correction when an established rule has been broken, the child learns that it is ok to break the rule. If you give in, this sends a message that the child can do whatever they want in life without consequence. You do not want to raise a child who will continually push boundaries and not follow commands. Needless to say, your child won't like all the rules you establish, but they are rules YOU establish. They don't have to like everything. Life will not always go their way. They must learn to live with the rules of society, starting with learning to live with the rules of your home.

A common point of friction with parents and children often occurs over picky eating. I have advised thousands of parents on this exact complaint. The key to avoiding picky eaters revolves around the establishment of the rules. First, you should offer a wide variety of foods with the introduction of solid foods in infancy. Keep giving the baby different foods including those they seem not to like much. As a result, they learn to eat all types of foods. In fact, with time they will like them more. Ensure that bottles have been phased out by age one as they cause tooth decay and tend to make children gain too much weight if they are always filled with juice or milk.

As a child ages, they will eat foods from all the food groups. If they don't, do not offer alternatives. If they refuse to eat what is on their plate, it is ok to let them not eat. A common trick used by young children is to fill up their bellies with juice or milk so that they don't feel the hunger. Make sure to give them water if they are thirsty, and leave the given food out for them to come back to later. Once they understand that you are not a short order chef and will not cook to order, they protest less about the food and simply eat it. You set the rules, you set the menu. It goes without saying that if they see you being picky, it will give them the perceived license to be picky themselves.

The meltdown can be the most feared response a child may give at this time. It is always held in the child's arsenal because it can get the quickest reaction out of a parent. This outburst should be handled the same way crying has been handled in the past. Ignore the situation. You must act like you see nothing wrong with your child. If they get any reaction from you, even a simple "stop it," they win and their behavior is reinforced. The outbursts may become longer and stronger before they figure out that it is not worth wasting all their energy since the tantrum gets nothing in return.

You must put aside the judgment of others. Strangers will always be willing to tell you how to raise your children. You cannot let that dissuade your intentions. They will judge you and give advice anyway. Those strangers, friends, and relatives are not the boss of your children.

You must not carry the guilt that makes you give into the tantrum. Those emotions must be put aside. Remember that your child is watching everything you do, and this shapes their behavior. If your child sees you yell, your child learns that yelling is acceptable. If your child sees you throw a tantrum, that gives the green light for tantrum throwing. Tantrums are very short-lived, although they seem like a lifetime when in public, when they are completely ignored. You can't show embarrassment or any inkling of emotion during the episode. Your child is intently watching you to see what they can get away with.

For instance, when I was still living in New York City as a pediatric resident, I often rode the train and bus to work. One morning on the 1st Avenue bus, I witnessed a young child go into a tantrum. The child was nearly three years old and was sitting next to his mother. He was dressed in a cute outfit consisting of jeans and a light blue oxford shirt, with the part in his hair brushed to the right complementing his big brown eyes. However, when he was enraged, he went into his best crying routine on this early morning rush hour accordion bus. He started screaming, but his mother ignored the protest. He screamed louder and tried to utter some incomprehensible words while crocodile tears gushed down his face. As his face reddened, his mother sat completely still and emotionless. The bus driver looked back in his mirror as people started shifting around on the bus, glaring at the mother, and passing judgment. People looked at the mother as if there was something they could do. I even saw a woman fishing around in her purse for a piece of candy to give to the child. Finally, there was no further recourse, the child threw himself onto the floor and screamed even louder. The mother, still emotionless, picked the child up from the floor (so he wouldn't be injured by the people standing on the bus) and let him continue to cry. He tried to throw himself down again, but the mom stood by her guns and emotionlessly held his arm so that he couldn't get away. Soon, the child began to settle down and it was my time to get off the bus at Bellevue. I exited out the back door and noticed that the mother got off through the front door with the child no longer crying. Although many people on that bus mumbled something under their breath or to each other about "shutting that kid up," I went to the mother, introduced myself, and told her what a wonderful job she did handling that tantrum. She politely smiled, thanked me, and went on her way inside of the hospital.

The point of the story is that tantrums can be very stressful, but you can't let the child rewrite the rules. You have to ignore both the tantrum and the observers while sticking to your rules. That is the quickest way to eliminate this behavior. You will soon find that your child will not have tantrums with you anymore. For other caretakers who have not mastered the art of ignoring your child's tantrums, they will continue with that individual. And while they are stressed out, you can bask in the glory of your success for a job well done. You may want to buy them a copy of this book and tell them what a great help it was to you.

Since getting your child to learn about consequences to negative or undesired behavior is essential, you can introduce the idea of penalties for bad behavior. Again, you must be consistent with enforcing the penalty when a negative behavior arises. Choosing not to enforce the penalty sometimes paves the way to more deviant behavior that further pushes the boundaries.

Gone are the days where you were told to go outside and pick up a switch for a spanking. Physical punishment is detrimental to the wellbeing of your child. Physical punishment is defined as abuse; you could risk losing your child.

Time out is the most widely accepted form of punishment for children of this age. Time out has proven to be an effective, non-detrimental form of punishment.

A general rule is to determine a place for the time out to occur--a certain room in the house, a rock or tree stump in the yard, or anywhere with minimal distractions. When your child violates the rules and the punishment is rendered, the child is sent to that place and given about 60-90 seconds for each year of age. Those minutes can seem like an eternity to the child, and with time it is effective in correcting their behavior. The key to this is the consistency of the enforcement for the rule infraction.

Alternatively, rewarding your child for good behavior is another way to encourage behavioral transformation. The star chart (described below) is effective for reinforcing good behaviors. When you reinforce good behaviors, the negative behaviors go away. This is also true for potty training. Reward the good conduct. At the end of the day, your child loves to see you smile and wants to please you.

If you are finding yourself struggling with bad behavior or you didn't have a chance to master the techniques discussed earlier (because I simply didn't get this book into your hands in time), try a star chart. The principle behind a star chart is that it sets up rewards for good behavior instead of penalties for bad behavior. A star chart is simply a piece of paper that you can hang up on a public place like the refrigerator. It is marked with the days of the week across the top. For each day there is the desired behavioral modification. For instance, for not talking out of turn place a star on the chart. Once the child has collected five stars they get a small prize or treat. The emphasis is small. You want to get something that won't break the budget. It could be a sticker or a trinket. If possible, try to avoid food as a reward as this could lead to problems with eating or obesity later in life. You must be able to provide the reward at every five-star moment. The praise must be given with exuberance. Conversely, a consequence chart can also be used for clearly defining the punishment for the behavioral infringement.

Continue to encourage your child to use their developing vocabulary to express emotions. Encourage verbal responses while discouraging emotional outbursts. This can set the stage for the open lines of communication you want to keep with your child for many years to come. With practice, you will master this stage of your child's development and be ready to take on the challenges that come with the next stage of their development, the school-aged years.

CHAPTER 4
School-Aged Children

By now, your child is ready to go off to school. Your child's great behavior at home will set them up to be the star of the class and the teacher's delight. This is a time where children learn more rules and expectations from school, their teacher, and sometimes (to our dismay) each other. This chapter will address some of the issues that come up in this age group. If you have had poor success with transforming your child's behavior up to this point, now is the time to get it under control.

As a review, the skills found in earlier chapters still apply. Setting the rules with expectations and enforcing them with time outs can be effective. Children learn largely by observation. You must set the good example. The faster they see no reaction to a negative behavior or tantrum, the quicker that negative action is extinguished.

This is the smartest your child has ever been. They have an understanding of time, and they know that they are way smarter now than they were as a baby. This leads to a more evolved and refined way of debating. Their negotiation skills have improved, but this does not mean that you have to give in. You have not been demoted; you are still the boss of your child. You should feel this way guilt free!

There are some helpful factors in this age group that further reinforce good behaviors in your child. Namely, sending your child off to school (even home school) has advantages. Now the child learns a new set of rules that are enforced by a different enforcer, the teacher. It is truly to your advantage to go and meet the teacher at parent conferences and other events. Then, you will have a better understanding of the expectations and rules during the school day. This way you can further align your rules with those of the school. The teacher will give you direct feedback on your child's behavior and you shouldn't hesitate to bring up any concerns with the teacher either.

If you pay attention to your child's behavior in school, you may wonder how the teacher got total control over your child in a couple of days when you haven't had control in five years. The key lies in enforcement of the rules. Many parents have complained that the kid listens to one parent while the other parent is ignored. Remember kids are smart. They get smarter daily. They will take the path of least resistance. If one parent always gives in, they know where to go.

In order to firm up your disciplinary muscle, you must back up what you threaten. Blind threats are the number one cause of dontlistentomomitis (this disease, first named by Doctor Jarret, is based upon children who don't listen to their mother). If you state as a disciplinary measure that you will not take your child to see that movie, don't. If you take your child anyway, the understanding is that the child gets their wants from Mommy no matter what. When you dish out a punishment, you think the punishment is against yourself. Stop the crazy thinking. Raising children is not all fun and games. Sometimes you have to make a sacrifice to gain the greater good (better behavior). You might have to miss that movie yourself, but think about how the sacrifice you make now will lead to better behavior in the future. That means less discipline in the future. That means less punishment. If you leave that child behind from the treat, the message becomes "Mommy does not play." They will think twice before disobeying.

Your child will be learning to read during these early school years. Continue to support that development with daily book reading time in addition to any other homework that is assigned. In fact, starting in about third grade, your child reads to learn. The fundamentals of reading can't be stressed enough, since schooling from that point forward is based upon reading. If your child struggles to read, they will struggle with virtually all subject matters going forward. Don't be afraid to request an evaluation of your child from the school, in writing, if you have concerns. Individualized Educational Plans (IEPs) are fundamental for any child with difficulties in school. This will keep them on track while getting the learning support they need.

Keeping your child active is another way that you can maintain the balance in their emotional development. Exercise is not only essential for fighting off the obesity epidemic, but improving emotional health also.

Children should get 60 minutes of exercise daily through play. This can include sports teams, but it does not have to be organized. Developing the habits of exercise early in life also sets it up to become a lifelong tradition. This reduces the likelihood of developing obesity and diabetes in childhood or early adulthood, helps the sleep cycle, and promotes emotional stability.

The improved observational skills of your child are being put to good use in school now. They will start to see things that they have never seen or done before. There will be kids in school that don't have the same conduct as your kids. They may hear profane language for the first time. They will try to use what they learn at school in the home. You must immediately convey the message that poor behavior will not be tolerated. The rules at home will remain enforced and the good behavior you have established will continue. Recall that positive incentives (by using the star chart described in the previous chapter) are still effective.

Another potential pitfall that begins in school is the concept of entitlement. Remember you are responsible for loving, clothing, feeding, and sheltering your child. You do not have to provide anything additional to them. They will hear stories and see things that other children have. Do not let this wreck your behavioral plan. Your child may feel deserving of things because some other child has them. This is simply not the case. If you start giving into your child's perceived entitlement now, it will persist and cost you plenty in the future (perhaps even throughout adulthood). You must have conversations about why something may not be appropriate for them. You may also need to explain why they can't have something. Financial education can never start too early. Responsible spending habits and the concept of needs and wants should be discussed to improve your child's future financial health.

Entitlement is real. You need to be aware of it and ensure that anything above and beyond the essentials are simply rewards for something such as good grades. Your child does not need to have an expensive pair of sneakers, but they do need to have a pair of sneakers. Just because little Johnny is allowed to play video games or watch movies that are not appropriate for young children does not entitle your child to do the same (more about this later).

Household chores can start to be implemented in this age group. Chores are a lesson of a skill and a responsibility, i.e., unloading the silverware out of the dishwasher. Living in your home should not come without cost, and assigning chores can be a way to show the young child a good work ethic. Naturally, they won't be capable of taking over chores entirely, but with your supervision they are able to learn the fundamentals of cleaning, cooking, and yard work. Modify and assign chores, like lining up the shoes next to the door, for them to be responsible for daily. Some chores should be done just as a part of what they do. Others can be done for a modest reward or payment as long as financial concepts like saving, spending, and obligations are being taught. As they get older, they will likely be able to contribute to the household chores with more efficiency and less pushback. They will understand family obligations and helping each other.

Schools tend to do a decent job of educating your child on several subjects you should also be talking about with them. Bullying, internet safety, and stranger danger are things you should discuss with your child. As they get more independence, they forget the basic lessons, i.e., look both ways before you cross the street. You must reinforce the safety lessons as well.

Bullying is something that happens despite the school's best efforts to thwart it, and it can discourage your child from doing the right thing. In fact, bullying is a learned behavior that can be perpetuated by your child if you are not continuing the lessons against it. This unfortunate tradition can also destroy the wellbeing of your child if they are victims. Parents, administrators, teachers, and communities must stand up against bullying.

Internet safety is also something that should be discussed. Your child's natural development continues with curiosity. As they learn to use computers, they get more exposure to media and games. Be sure to monitor what your child is searching for and playing on the internet. There are many predators out there that may try to befriend your child. It is important to set limits on what can be done and what should not be done on the computer. In addition, you should have all of the passwords to their electronic devices and applications. It seems like you are invading their privacy, but it is all about safety.

Furthermore, video game rating systems aren't simply for decoration. Please read them and adhere to them. I have seen way too many four to eight-year-olds playing games designed for adults than I care to mention. The violence, sex, and drug innuendos in these games can be overwhelming, confusing, and at the very least stressful for your child. Those are all topics for discussion with you, their parent, as they get older. They should not learn about prostitution while playing on their favorite game console. The same is true for movies. PG-13 and R-rated movies should largely be left out of the young school-aged child's vocabulary. If they must be watched, it should be done with the parents. Violence, sex, tobacco, alcohol, and drugs should be addressed so the child has no misunderstanding of social norms. Hollywood and digital media have a very strong and impressionable effect. Without guidance, digital media will dictate the values and morals of your child.

Sleep can be overlooked as a cause of poor behavior. School-aged children need nine to twelve hours of sleep every night. This means that they need to get to sleep relatively early for an early morning start for school. However, it is not only the quantity of sleep that counts, it is the quality. Children need a proper area for sleeping. The sleep environment should be free of televisions, cell phones, and other electronic gadgets. The room should also be quiet and dark. Distractions from televisions and cell phones can disrupt the sleep. When sleep is disrupted, proper rest can't be attained. When there is not enough rest, behavior issues are among the first to surface.

Finally, nutrition is not something that can be neglected at this time. An improper diet can contribute to poor behavior. Although poor eating habits can be well formed by this age, children do not have to continue to eat in that manner. Let's start by reviewing what they should be eating. 5-4-3-2-1-0 is still the standard. They should have 5 servings of fruits and vegetables daily, followed by 4 servings of carbohydrates (carbs), 3 servings of dairy, 2 servings of proteins, 1 junk food, and 0 sodas or juice daily. Recall that you have to provide food to your child, not food that they like. You would be surprised what your child eats when they simply have no choice in food, and what they drink when water is their only option and they are not allowed to fill up on milk or juice. Stand strong and you will see. Keep the observational skills in mind of this age group, and remember that they will wonder why you don't eat the same way they do.

School adds new challenges to your parenting plan. Tempering entitlement, safety reinforcement, proper sleep, and proper nutrition will firm up good behavior. You are well on your way to having a well-developed tween and teen.

CHAPTER 5

Tweens and Teens

If this is only the second chapter you have read in this book, all is not lost. You still have hope for transforming your child. In this stage, your child has had the advantage of several years of schooling to learn from others (good and bad) and has become smarter and more rational. They are now the smartest that they have ever been. This makes them feel like they are ready to be in charge. Wait, you are still responsible for paying the rent, clothing, and feeding them. This does not make them in charge. To make things more complicated, hormonal changes that occur in this time period compound the behavior and their thought process. This is a time of rapid growth and change that can wreak havoc on your child and their behavior, even if they have been well behaved until this point.

The basic principles are the same for this age group as they were during previous years. You are responsible for loving them while giving them needs. You are not to carry around guilt regarding anything in their life (or your own for that matter) that has the potential to affect them negatively. You want the best for your kids, but that doesn't mean that you have to give it to them. They must earn it in some way.

School is their primary responsibility at this age. Academics must take precedence over everything else, even that illustrious football career that has them on a path to the NFL. As a parent, setting up academic goals is important, as this will lead your child to college and perhaps scholarship opportunities. Helping them to establish a routine early on will allow them to understand that their top priority is school, and that before play is when to get their work done. With longer projects like the science fair, work with your child to help them establish their own deadlines. This facilitates their learning about working on a schedule and not waiting until the last minute. You can leverage academic success to just about any want your child has. Your reward system for good behavior can surround academic achievement. This encourages motivation while reducing entitlement.

Chores can now be the mainstay of the t(w)een family participation. They are now old enough to fully participate in the household chores—cooking, laundry, cleaning, dishes, yard work, and much more. The lesson here is not that you can get free labor (although that is a good side effect). Chores should be a lesson in working together, helping and responsibility, along with the skills that are learned, i.e., how to mow the lawn. If an allowance or stipend for chores is given, you must accompany the money with financial lessons about saving, obligations, and consumerism. Of course, this is the age where the most expensive toys, clothing, and other wants occur. Saving or giving a strict budget for some of it will go a long way in teaching financial responsibility.

In the previous chapter, we discussed entitlement and ways in which you can temper it. Entitlement can be very strong at this age, and continued exposure to other children increases it. Often, kids think that everything is simply given to them, and the difficult part is that many times things ARE. They will walk through life thinking that everything is supposed to happen that way. But, the sense of responsibility given by chores helps to alleviate entitlement.

T(w)eens have the desire to be considered young adults. However, they don't fit in. They are often annoyed by younger children while they don't have the wisdom to fit in with adults. This leaves them to socialize as a group, often through social media. Giving them increased responsibility at home and granting them some independence over their schedule helps them to fulfill this desire.

Many other parents don't take the time to put their own kids in check. This makes your child question, by comparison, the rules at home. They put their brains to work trying to figure out ways to outsmart or outmaneuver a parent in order to have personal gain. They can be slick because as a parent you still see that cute baby face even though that baby face may have a beard growing on it.

Hormonal changes in this age group are responsible for many different features of the t(w)een group. First, the changes in puberty occur at this time. Pubertal changes can make boys and girls more self-conscious of their bodies. For example, girls fixate on their curves or lack thereof, and boys often focus on their muscles. Along with the hair, odor, and acne changes that come during this time, emotional instability can also occur. It is essential that as a parent you are in tune with your child's emotional change and development because often they hide it from you. Although your child's doctor should be screening them for depression in this age group, pay attention because with the influence of social media, t(w)eens are particularly vulnerable as their self-confidence can be low.

These hormonal changes also alter their appetite and eating habits. The BMI (Body Mass Index) becomes harder to change in this age group. If they are thin, they might remain thin as long as proper nutrition is maintained. If your child is overweight or obese, now is the time that they might pack on extra pounds (even before they head to college for those "freshman fifteen" pounds). T(w)eens have very picky and poor eating habits. Remember that your t(w)een will observe your eating and exercise habits as well. Be sure to set a good example. Sixty minutes of daily exercise should still be a goal for all.

Although it is best to establish healthy eating habits early in life, even during infancy, getting your t(w)een to eat healthily is still achievable. Nutrition is often based on convenience to food. If your pantry is filled with cookies and snack cakes, that will be what your child goes for. You must primarily have healthy options in the house. Keep lots of fresh fruits, veggies, and nuts around for your child to snack on. This will satiate the appetite, which can be ravenous during the growth spurts, and allow for healthy eating. With primarily healthy food choices, hunger will win. The child will snack on an apple, sometimes reluctantly, because that is the only available and convenient snack. You provide the food, and it is your duty to provide the nutrition. You can be in charge of menu planning. There is no room for guilt from you or entitlement from them.

The other nutritional item that leads to extra pounds in this age group comes by way of what they drink. Sports drinks, soda, flavored milk, and even 100 percent juice (let alone anything less than 100 percent) should not be routine drink options. By routine, I mean more than three times a week. About 16 ounces of low fat (unflavored) milk should be consumed daily, and for all other thirst options plain water should be the choice. Several eight-ounce portions of water should be consumed daily, more when they are athletically active. There is no need for sports drinks or sodas at this time. The soda and sports drink market makes millions of dollars from good marketing. They make it seem as if you are losing gallons of electrolytes when you sweat; but, your body is actually pretty good at saving what you need (even though your sweat tastes salty). For example, most Americans consume way more than the recommended amount of sodium. This means that most have a plentiful supply in their bodies.

Sleep is also affected by these pesky hormonal changes. The natural clock of the t(w)een starts to tick longer into the night. They are more inclined to stay awake later at night despite having earlier school start times. Proper sleep hygiene is again the key to developing good sleeping habits. At night, at least 30 minutes prior to bedtime, make sure that the electronic devices are removed from their possession. This includes tablets, cell phones, televisions, and computers. Using these devices right before bed tends to disrupt the relaxation prior to sleep onset. Their brains are stimulated and activated from the electronics. Typically, these devices shouldn't be stored in the child's room because of the temptation to get them in the middle of the night, which establishes a poor sleep routine. They still need eight to ten hours of sleep nightly; however, with activities and homework this can be difficult to accomplish.

Hormonal changes and peer pressure can lead to risky behavior. In order to keep good behavior and avoid risky behavior, having open preventive conversation is necessary. Frank discussions about alcohol, drugs, sex, and tobacco are essential. These conversations should start in the early t(w)eens (perhaps as young as 10 years old) and continue throughout high school. Having these discussions in addition to having regular family time (like a family dinner) helps to reduce addictive behaviors and teen pregnancy.

Finally, emotions can run high during this period. Everything, particularly things that seem small to us adults, can mean the end of the world to the t(w)een. It is important, however, not to let the child run the household with their "sass mouth." If the tendencies of the child are to be defiant or disrespectful to the parent or another adult, immediate measures must be taken starting with a discussion of what is not tolerated. This can be reinforced with a written set of rules. The written rules make it easier to refer to when there is an infraction. A consequence chart can state the rule and the penalty for the infraction. The penalties can be simple, i.e., take away the cell phone for a certain amount of time, extra chores, or cancel an upcoming social event. However, the action must be swift. The longer you allow the negative behavior, the longer it will persist. When they know you mean business, the behavior will extinguish.

At this time, you have managed to develop a well-behaved, well-rounded t(w)een. However, your work is not done. Continue reading to discover the techniques for handling the young adult.

CHAPTER 6

Young Adults

Now, your precious baby has graduated from high school and is off to start the next part of their life in college or at work. This doesn't mean your job as a parent is done. This time can be particularly troubling because the temptation for you to not let them fail can stifle their development. In the age of "helicopter parents" and "smother mother's," it is important to remember a few things about this age group.

Young adulthood is extended adolescence. Women take until their early-20s and men may take up to their mid-20s to complete adolescence. This means that their minds are still developing, and they might make mistakes. It is crucial that you let them figure out and correct their own mistakes at this time, or they are at risk for never having problem-solving skills. As parents, we are tempted to jump in at the first signs of trouble to correct the course of action and save our babies. However, your child will not learn if they are not left to figure it out. You always want to be of help because you love your children, but you must learn to step away.

At this time, your obligation to feed, shelter, and clothe them starts to fade. At the same time, your love remains just as strong as ever. However, you can't let your love interfere with their independence. After all, you do want them to move out of the house at some point.

These days it is not uncommon for your child to want to move back home. Often, it is from having financial difficulty or problems finding employment. There is nothing wrong with having them move back in, but beware. Before they come home, you should set up a contract of expectations with them. Nothing is off limits—curfew, contribution to bills, grocery shopping, visitors, and more. You should review your expectations with your adult child prior to them moving back home. This will give them an understanding of what is expected. You may not want your child wandering in and out of your house with frequent guests and hosting parties. That is why a contract should be written. This will be much like any other list of expectations they had in their previous residence. Remember their entitlement will be soaring at an all-time high.

You don't want to make your home too comfortable for them. If they live with accommodations that include a chef and a maid, they may never move out. (P.S. let me know where you live. I will sign up!) Consider having them pay for a portion of the household expenses. This helps them learn to pay "rent." With this "rent," feel free to treat yourself or save it for them. The "rent" they pay may add up to an amount they can put down on their new apartment or townhome. This will help get them on their way out.

If things break down with the contract you negotiated, pull it out and attempt to repair the damage. Having a series of conversations should rectify the problem. However, if things continue to be bad, you may need to force them out. This seems like a harsh move, but your child will continue to learn lessons in life and this is another one.

In the end, they are still your children. Watching them fail can be very difficult. However, with failure comes success. This is no time for guilt, as you have prepared them the best way you know how. They will be stronger and better adults because of you. They will also learn to be better parents to their own children as they build on the start you have given them. Let them go and let them grow!

EPILOGUE

Thank you for reading my book! You are now equipped with some of the skills that will help you have more success rearing your child(ren). I wrote this book with the desire to help parents take better care of their kids. Doctors are busy, and in today's clinical practices there is little time to discuss things of importance to the parent. I know because I always ran late on my schedule because of trying to give parents what they wanted. Even though my clinical practice has changed, I still want parents to get what they need.

Hopefully, with time, you will see your child grow in independence. The series of lessons that you have taught them through the ages will pay off. They will be able to take care of themselves through the lessons of chores, work, ethics, economics, nutrition, and many others. If you have young children and have a long time to go, feel free to reference this book when you need to. The lessons build and repeat so that you can continue your effective parenting.

You can also find helpful parenting information on my Facebook page. It is a way to connect with me and follow my live streams.

Like me at www.facebook.com/DoctorJarret

ABOUT THE AUTHOR

Jarret "Doctor Jarret" Patton, MD, a board-certified pediatrician with nearly 20 years of experience, spent his clinical career taking care of children in an urban clinic and his administrative career as a top physician executive in eastern Pennsylvania. After earning his bachelor of science in chemistry from Xavier University of Louisiana, he went on to earn his doctor of medicine at Case Western Reserve University.

Doctor Jarret now provides transformative relationship advice for hospitals, physicians, parents, and children through education, motivation, and empowerment. His pediatric influence reaches far and wide, as he has frequently been featured in print, online, radio, and television media, and is the bestselling author of *Licensed to*

Live. In addition to writing books, he runs a physician coaching program and consultation firm to further improve healthcare on a larger scale.

Doctor Jarret resides in Reading, Pennsylvania, with his wife and three children.

To connect, visit his website at
www.doctorjarret.com